Farm Animals

Chickens

Rachael Bell

Heinemann
LIBRARY

The author would like to thank Patrick Edwards and hopes Harry and George enjoy reading about their farm.

First published in Great Britain by Heinemann Library
Halley Court, Jordan Hill, Oxford OX2 8EJ,
a division of Reed Educational and Professional Publishing Ltd.
Heinemann is a registered trademark of Reed Educational & Professional Publishing Limited.

OXFORD MELBOURNE AUCKLAND
JOHANNESBURG BLANTYRE GABORONE
IBADAN PORTSMOUTH NH (USA) CHICAGO

Designed by AMR
Originated by Ambassador Litho Ltd
Printed in Hong Kong/China

04 03 02 01 00
10 9 8 7 6 5 4 3 2 1

ISBN 0 431 10085 3

British Library Cataloguing in Publication Data
Bell, Rachael, 1972–
  Chickens. – (Farm animals)
  1.Chickens – Juvenile literature
  I.Title
  636.5

Acknowledgements
The Publishers would like to thank the following for permission to reproduce photographs:
Agripicture/Peter Dean p 24; Anthony Blake Picture Library p 21, 23; Bruce Coleman pp 5/Jane Burton; Farmers Weekly Picture Library p 20; Holt Studios pp 4/Sarah Rowland, 10/Michael Mayer, 11, 25 & 27/Inga Spence, 12 & 18/Gordon Roberts, 14/Bjorn Ullhagen, 15/Richard Anthony, 17 & 28/Nigel Cattlin; Chris Honeywell p 22; Images of Nature/FLPA pp 6/Peter Dean, 8 & 9/Gerard Lacz; NHPA p 26/ Joe Blossom; Photo Researchers Inc p 19/Kenneth H Thomas; Roger Scruton p 29; Lynn Stone pp 7, 13; Tony Stone Images pp 16/Tony Page.

Cover photograph reproduced with permission of The Stock Market.

Our thanks to Tony Prior, Bowers Farm, Wantage, Oxon, for his comments in the preparation of this book.

Every effort has been made to contact copyright holders of any material reproduced in this book. Any omissions will be rectified in subsequent printings if notice is given to the Publisher.

For more information about Heinemann Library books, or to order, please phone 01865 888066, or send a fax to 01865 314091. You can visit our web site at www.heinemann.co.uk

Contents

Words printed in bold **like this** are
explained in the Glossary.

Chicken relatives

Chickens are farm birds that come in many sizes and colours. These red chickens are good at **laying** lots of eggs.

Farm chickens are related to wild chickens that still live in the jungles of Asia. Wild chickens fly up into trees at night to keep out of danger.

Welcome to the chicken farm

On this farm there are hundreds of **free range** chickens in a grassy field. They are very friendly. When they see people, they think they are going to be fed!

This farmer also keeps a few **beef cattle**. He buys young **calves** and then feeds them up. He sells them for their meat when they are fully grown.

Meet the chickens

tail

ear
(it is just
a hole)

nostril

beak

wing

leg

The **female** chicken is called a hen.
She **lays** about six eggs. Then she sits
on them for 21 days, to keep them
warm until they **hatch**.

comb

wattle

spur

foot
(four
toes)

The **male** is called a cock, or rooster. He is bigger than the hen and has a larger **comb** and **wattle**. His feathers are more colourful. He likes to show off and **crow** very loudly!

Meet the baby chicken

Because chicks come out of an egg, they have a special egg-tooth on their beak. It helps them break out of the shell. Chicks have fine, fluffy **down**, so they keep warm under their mother.

Chicks make a 'cheep cheep' sound. The hen teaches them to feed. She pecks at food, then drops it for the chicks to eat. They copy her and learn to peck.

Where do chickens live?

On this farm, the chickens live in hen houses. These stand in a large field of grass. There is an electric fence over one metre high to stop foxes getting in.

Each house has a thick layer of **shavings** on the floor. This keeps the chickens' feet clean and dry. Each house has egg boxes. The farmer opens them from outside to collect the eggs.

What do chickens eat?

Chickens peck at anything to see if it is worth eating. They eat plants, seeds, earth, insects and worms. They have no teeth and cannot chew so they eat **grit**. It grinds up the food in their stomachs.

On this farm, the chickens peck at the grass. They also eat wheat and a **cereal** mix called **layers mash** from a **trough**. They have water drinkers too.

How do chickens stay healthy?

Chickens scratch the ground to find food. They need plenty of ground to run about and scratch in. They prefer grass, as it keeps their feet clean.

Chickens **preen** to keep their feathers clean. They comb them with their beaks. They also take dust baths. This gets rid of **parasites** and helps them stay cool.

How do chickens sleep?

Young chicks sleep under their mother during the day and at night. She fluffs up her feathers to let them all under. She can sit on as many as 20 chicks!

Like other birds, chickens roost at night. Their feet can lock onto a branch or a **rod**. The chickens will not fall off, even when they are asleep!

Who looks after the chickens?

The farmer opens up the hen houses as soon as it is light. In the evening, he closes them again. He also tops up the food and water.

It is a lot of work to **rear** hens, so this farmer buys his hens from someone else. He buys them at four months old, just before they start **laying** eggs.

What are chickens kept for?

The hens on this farm are kept for the eggs they **lay**. The farm produces about 500 eggs every day. They are sold for people to eat. Eggs are also used in many foods, like cakes.

Chickens are also kept for their meat. Chicken can be roasted whole or in pieces. The meat can also be chopped up and used in many different dishes.

Other kinds of chicken farm

Some big chicken farms sell thousands of eggs a day. They keep their hens inside. They cannot scratch, run in grass or take dust baths.

Most of the chicken meat we buy comes from big farms. They keep lots of **broiler chickens** inside. These grow big very quickly. Some are ready for eating at six weeks old!

More chicken farms

Some farms **rear** many different types of chickens. You can go and choose the kind of chickens you want to keep. They may also sell hen houses.

Some special farms only rear chicks
to sell to other farmers. These farms
often use machines to **incubate**
the eggs.

Fact file

 Chicks have fine, fluffy **down**. They keep warm under their mother. The chicks start to lose their fluffy down at two to three weeks. They replace it with more adult feathers by about five weeks. They **moult** these when they are over a year old. The chick becomes an adult when it is about five months old.

 Chickens have special **organs** in their legs that can feel tiny **vibrations** in the ground. They can feel any enemy coming towards them long before they can see them.

Chickens have a strict **pecking order**. If there is one cock and lots of hens, he is the most important chicken. He chases any other cocks away. The hens peck at each other to find out who comes next, right down to the last one. If a hen goes, or new ones join them, they have to find out who is boss all over again!

The hen which laid the most eggs was a White Leghorn from the USA. In 1978 she laid 371 eggs!

Glossary

beef cattle   name given to cows and bulls that are kept for their meat

broiler chickens   young chickens grown for meat

calves   young cows or bulls. You say one calf, many calves.

cereal   wheat, oats and barley, often made into breakfast food

comb   skin flap on top of the chicken's head

crow   loud call or screech that a hen or cock makes

down   fluffy covering that newly-hatched birds have

female   the girl or mother

free range   animals that are mostly kept outside and have plenty of space

grit   tiny crumbs of stone or shell

hatch   break out of the egg

incubate   keep eggs warm so that they hatch

lay   produce an egg that the baby chick will hatch from

layers mash   special food for laying hens made of different cereals. Farmers buy it already mixed.

male	the boy or father
moult	lose feathers or hair. They often grow back.
organs	special parts of the body
parasites	tiny animals that live on other bigger animals and usually harm them
pecking order	chickens find out who is boss by pecking at each other
preen	what birds do to keep their feathers in good condition
rear	bring up young animals or children
rod	thin, straight stick or bar
shavings	very thin strips cut from wood
trough	special food container that stops the food being spilled out, or any straw or rats getting in
vibrations	tiny, fast movements that can sometimes be felt from a distance
wattle	flap of skin that hangs from the chin of a chicken

More books to read

Story books
Queenie the Bantam, Walker Books
Little Chick, Walker Books

Information books
Life Cycle of a Chicken, Heinemann Library
Animal Young – Birds, Heinemann Library
The Farming Year, Autumn, Winter, Spring, Summer,
  Wayland
Mealtimes – Evening Meals Around the World,
  Wayland

Index